WHO SHOULD I

· · · · · · · · · · · · · · · · · ·

Listen To?

Early Teen Devotionals
by Kevin Johnson

Can I Be a Christian Without Being Weird?

Why Is God Looking For Friends?

Who Should I Listen To?

WHO SHOULD I

KEVIN JOHNSON

BETHANY HOUSE PUBLISHERS
MINNEAPOLIS, MINNESOTA 55438

Published by Bethany House Publishers
A Ministry of Bethany Fellowship, Inc.
11300 Hampshire Avenue South
Minneapolis, Minnesota 55438

Printed in the United States of America

Library of Congress Cataloging-in-Publication Data

Johnson, Kevin. (Kevin Walter)
   Who should I listen to? / Kevin Johnson
      p.   cm.

    1. Junior high school students—Prayer-books and
devotions—English. 2. Teenagers—Prayer-books and
devotions—English. [1. Prayer books and devotions.
2. Christian life.] I. Title.
BV4850.J647   1993
242'.63—dc20   93-37743
                                        CIP
ISBN 1–55661–283–4   AC

To Nate

May you always hear
God's kind voice
echoed in mine.

KEVIN JOHNSON is an associate pastor at Elmbrook Church in metro Milwaukee, where he works with almost 400 sixth–eighth graders. While his training includes an M.Div. from Fuller Theological Seminary and a B.A. in English and Print Journalism from the University of Wisconsin at River Falls, his current interests run along the lines of cycling, in-line skating, books, guitar, and shortwave radio. Kevin and his wife, Lyn, live in Wisconsin with their two children, Nathaniel and Karin.

Contents

Part 1: Sortin' Out the Chaos

1. Who Do You Listen To? 11
2. School Pictures 15
3. Nowhere to Hide 17
4. Masterpiece 19
5. Yeehaw 21
6. The Sign 23
7. Inside the Palace 25
8. The Ultimate Coach 27
9. You Belong on the Bomb Squad 29
10. He Has Plans for You 31
11. No Lie 33

Part 2: Hangin' on the Vine

12. Bewildered No More 37
13. Twinkies for Lunch 39
14. Give Me the Light 41
15. Not That Dumb 43
16. Pink Bunny Sheets 45
17. He Treats You Right 47
18. Don't They Get It? 49
19. After the Funeral 51

20. Stinky Feet 53
21. Here Kitty, Kitty 55
22. Resolutions.................................. 57
23. A Promise or a Threat? 59

Part 3: Livin' Under Heaven

24. Is God a Wimp? 63
25. The Jester.................................... 65
26. He Doesn't Wear Red Tights 67
27. The Art of Self-Defense 69
28. Stupid Rocks................................. 71
29. In a Coffin................................... 73
30. Mutant Librarian's Daughters 75
31. Not Just on Mother's Day.................... 77
32. Only If You Do What We Want................ 79
33. Rulebusters 81
34. Swine Diving................................. 83
35. Lemmings and Lerts......................... 85

Part 4: Searchin' the Mirror

36. You're So Gullible............................ 89
37. Truth in a Toilet............................. 91
38. Your Hand Looks Dead 93
39. Just in Case.................................. 95
40. Wasted Waiting............................. 97
41. But He Said He Loves Me 99
42. It Makes a Poor Parachute 101
43. When Truth Clashes.........................103
44. Stargazing 105
45. Get Smart...................................107
46. Morning Breath 109

PART 1

Sortin' out the CHAOS

1
Who Do You Listen To?

ACT I, Scene 3

COACH: (*whacks Josh with a baseball hat*) It was a simple tag. What happened? The throw was right on your glove. How could you drop the ball? *You* lost the game!

TEACHER: (*pats Josh on the head*) Josh, your report was outstanding. You're far, far ahead of your peers in intelligence. You are really quite remarkable.

GIRLFRIEND: (*runs fingers through hair*) Oooh, you're such a hunk. Hey—I know your parents don't want you to—but meet me after school, okay?

MOVIE: (*A gigantic screen behind Josh lights up. An automatic rifle burps, splattering bullets into a crowd. Bodies thud as they hit the ground.*)

MOTHER: (*smothers Josh with a hug*) My poor baaaaby! Those other kids hit you first, right? I know you would never, ever pick a fight.

FATHER: (*shakes an angry finger at Josh*) You got a C in math? You might as well have gotten an F! When *I* was your age *I* did better. You're not living up to your potential.

KID: (*holds out a mix he has been inhaling*) Whatsamatter? You afraid or something? Don't be such a nerd.

TV SET: (*A TV rolls in from stage left and smashes into

Josh's legs. A commercial is on. Beauteous guys and girls leap and dive in a game of beach volleyball. Everyone breaks to slug down a cold beer.)

FRIEND: (*pulls on Josh's sleeve*) Come on! Let's skip class. The Fat Lady is *sooooo* boring. Besides, you don't think . . .

(*Suddenly, all the lights go out. The stage is lit only by the movie screen, and everyone begins talking at once.*) HOW COULD YOU? YOU'RE REALLY QUITE RE-MARKABLE! MEET ME AFTER SCHOOL, OKAY? MY POOR BAAAABY! YOU'RE NOT LIVING UP TO YOUR POTENTIAL. DON'T BE SUCH A NERD. LET'S CUT CLASS. IT'S SOOOO BORING.

Amidst the noise Josh collapses to the floor.

You're like Josh. You can't escape hearing dozens of voices—family, school, friends, media, even your maturing body and brain—telling you every day what to do.

You're surrounded.

With so many voices screaming at you, which ones do you believe? How do you know who is wrong—or who is right? Who speaks truth? Who spouts lies?

Who should you listen to?

The easy way is to give up and follow whichever voice is the loudest.

That isn't the only way. Jesus invites you to follow Him, wanting you to answer to His voice. He helps you sort out the other voices. He shows you truth from lies, good from bad, real from fake.

This book will help you hear Jesus' voice—*God's voice*—by getting you into the Bible.

Read a chapter at a sitting, one a day if you can. You'll need to bring a Bible—find one that's easy to read—so you can look up the Bible passage where it says ☑ **Read**, and check out exactly what God says. You can find out more by reading the verses that pop up in parentheses, and you may want to memorize some of the verses at the end of each chapter—so you can remember word for word what God says to you.

God's voice isn't the loudest, because He respects you too much to scream at you.

But listen up. You'll discover that He's the One worth listening to.

2

School Pictures

Merri opened her envelope of school pictures and gasped. Last year's picture was bad enough, but this year's—uggh! Her bangs looked more tortured than teased, her left eye was half shut, and her face looked like she had rammed her nose against the camera lens.

Her friend Brandi pretended to hide her own packet. Merri grabbed it, hoping someone else's picture looked as bad.

"Promise not to laugh, okay?" Brandi begged Merri. "I look awful!" Yeah right. Brandi's photo glowed like a model's, and Brandi knew it.

Brandi pulled out Merri's picture. "Ooooh. Merri, Merri," she said sadly. She peeked again and handed the packet back. "I'm so sorry. Bad hair day, huh?"

That night in her room Merri studied her face in a mirror, wondering one thing: *Do I really look like my school picture?*

📖 **Read Psalm 139:23–24. How do you get an accurate picture of yourself?**

Some days you might think you look like a poster child for Uglies Anonymous. That's not likely. If you actually looked as doofy as most school pictures, you

15

would probably go through life with a paper sack over your head.

Yet if you can't trust a photograph, how do you find out what you really look like on the outside—or more importantly, on the inside?

People's opinions can be wrong. An enemy won't paint a pretty picture: "Whadja do to your hair?" or "Nobody likes you" or "You goody-goody." The portrait friends paint of you can be just the opposite—*too* pretty, like an air-brushed photo with all the zits gone: "It wasn't your fault at all" or "You're a perfect friend" or "Don't ever change."

The writer of Psalm 139 knew that only God—who knows us inside and out, even better than we know ourselves—sees us the way we really are. He prayed that God would examine his words, attitudes, and actions, and show him the ugly parts of his life. Then God could make those parts better.

Being happy with yourself and being willing to let God fix the uglies only starts when you see yourself honestly.

And it's God's view of you that's true.

———

Search me, O God, and know my heart; test me and know my anxious thoughts. See if there is any offensive way in me, and lead me in the way everlasting.

PSALM 139:23–24

3
Nowhere to Hide

No. Your stomach knots. *They didn't.* You were only gone a minute. *No! They couldn't have!* They did. They left without you.

Everyone from the school ski club had loaded up to go skiing, but you figured you had time to run to the bathroom. When you came out, everyone had left. Not one person missed you.

What do I do now? I could call home and congratulate Dad and Mom on being proud parents of a reject—maybe the school has a bumper sticker they can put on the car to tell everyone. No, wait. I could roll outside in the snow, get all wet, hide in the bathroom for the next six hours, and emerge just as everyone gets back. If I play it right, I can make everyone believe I went with them. Yeah, that's the plan.

📝 **Read Psalm 139:1–10. Where could you go so God couldn't find you?**

God always has His eye on you, but sometimes you don't want to be seen.

You might be terrified to realize that God knows everything you think, hears everything you say, and sees everything you do. You might feel like a criminal suspect—bugged, followed, and photographed by the

FBI—or like a convict tracked by a radio transmitter welded to his ankle. Nowhere to hide.

It doesn't have to feel that way. God's knowing you totally means He always knows where you are. He knows trivial things like the weight of the lint in your belly button and the progress of the pimple you've been tracking. It also means He knows huge things like your problems, hurts, and needs. Because God knows you completely, He can guide you with perfect wisdom. Because God is everywhere, you can rest in His protection.

God isn't the FBI, or Santa Claus making a list and checking it twice. He isn't like a teacher who leaves a tape recorder running when she leaves the room to catch her students goofing off. God doesn't spy. He cares. He says that you matter, especially to Him.

He's the best friend who's always right beside you, who will never drive off without you.

You know when I sit and when I rise; you perceive my thoughts from afar. You discern my going out and my lying down; you are familiar with all my ways.

PSALM 139:2–3

4
Masterpiece

"Brandon! Jeremy! Tadd! Andy!" The cabin counselor jarred his campers awake. "Get dressed! Gentlemen, we're going for a hike." At first the guys wondered why Jason was rousing them at three in the morning on the last night of camp. Then they worried about what he might have planned to retaliate for their obnoxiousness that week.

The four of them stumbled through the forest behind Jason until they stopped at the shore of a lake. The sky had exploded with stars.

Jason told them to sit down and enjoy the view. It was the first time they had shut up all week. "Makes you feel small, doesn't it?" Jason asked after a few minutes. The guys stayed quiet. Jason waited a bit before he said more. "God painted an incredible sky, didn't He? But it's nothing compared to what God made when He sculpted you. You guys need to stop acting like dirtballs. That's not who you are."

▶ **Read Psalm 8:1–9. What does God think of the people He made?**

Bragging—that your high jumps are higher, your grades greater, your clothes classier, your looks more luscious—is pointless: God owns everything. He's the best at everything. And we don't have anything good that didn't come from Him (1 Corinthians 4:7). Compared to God, the Maker and Master of everything, we're tiny mudsplats.

Yet that isn't how God thinks about human beings. He created us so that we would reflect His greatness the way the moon—which makes no light of its own—reflects the light of the sun. He gave each of us the privilege of knowing, obeying, and worshiping Him, the God of the universe. He made human beings responsible for ruling our world.

Those aren't jobs He would give to mudsplats.

You probably look at stuff you make—a clay pot in art class, a napkin holder from shop, a report for English—and think it's stupid. But God was very pleased when He made you (Genesis 1:31).

So you're more than mud. You're God's masterpiece.

When I consider your heavens, the work of your fingers, the moon and the stars, which you have set in place, what is man that you are mindful of him?

PSALM 8:3—4

5
Yeehaw

Through thin walls Courtney heard what she wasn't supposed to hear. The school counselor told her parents that if Courtney's work didn't improve, she would have to do seventh grade over.

Her parents' response burned in her mind. "We realize she's had problems," they apologized. "She's a little slow."

Slow? Courtney thought. *Why don't they just call me "stupid," like the kids do?*

At that moment Courtney decided she would never let anyone say she was dumb ever again. She started studying with a flashlight under her blankets late at night, and setting her alarm for five A.M. She wanted the highest grade in every class. A *95* wasn't good enough; she chewed herself out for not scoring *100.*

✔ **Read Jeremiah 9:23–24. What should the goal of your life be?**

You probably like being laughed at: *You waddle when you run. You wear that shirt all the time. Your answer was stupid. You sweat buckets when you talk in front of class.*

Probably not.

Nothing is wrong with wanting to run faster, score

21

higher, dress neater, or speak sweeter. There's a problem, though, if you think that winning the race, making your bangs look perfect, or never wearing the same outfit twice makes you valuable and acceptable to yourself, to others, or to God.

There's a problem when those things matter more than anything else—then you've stopped chasing a good goal, and instead you're *being chased*—by a wild-eyed cowboy wielding a sizzling branding iron. When you think that brains, bucks, and beauty are the most important things you could ever possess, you know you've been branded with an attitude that doesn't come from God. You've been burned.

The *best* goal to chase is to know God and to like what He likes. To God, your insides matter more than your outsides (1 Samuel 16:7).

"Let him who boasts boast about this: that he understands and knows me, that I am the Lord, who exercises kindness, justice and righteousness on earth, for in these I delight," declares the Lord.

JEREMIAH 9:24

6
The Sign

A cold night rain pelts the rebel encampment outside the king's palace. You and a dozen other guerrillas warm yourself near a fire, waiting for your only meal of the day—tree bark soup.

Years of fighting have made you both tough and tired. Through the palace gates you can see bright lights and hear what sounds like a party. A sign on the gate reads WELCOME. LEAVE YOUR WEAPONS OUTSIDE. ROYAL FEAST AT MIDNIGHT. COME EARLY.

"What do you think the sign means?" you wonder out loud.

"It's exactly what we're fighting against," your commander hisses. "The sign is a lie! The king hates us. Why else would we be out here starving?"

"So why aren't the gates locked?" you ask.

"It's a trick. A trap." Your commander's bitterness makes you shiver. "You're not starting to believe the sign, are you?" He swings his automatic rifle around and shreds the sign with a spray of bullets. "Tomorrow we try again to storm the palace."

☛ **Read Psalm 5:4–8. What does God think about those who rebel against Him?**

Some enemies of God are easy to spot, as though they carry bazookas. Their wrongdoing—their sin—is obvious: They fight, kill, lie, or steal. They misuse sex. They disobey parents and beat up brothers and sisters. Or they hurt their own bodies by drinking or abusing drugs.

The sins of other people are harder to see. Even nice people with polite outsides, the Bible says, can have rotted insides. They may have a bad attitude toward God—by refusing to bow before His greatness or to applaud His absolute goodness. People make their own plans for life and mistrust God's wisdom. By that standard, God says that *all* human beings have messed up and sinned—including you. We're all rebels (Romans 3:23).

God can't stand evil. As rebels we have been kicked out of the palace (Genesis 3:22–24). But God doesn't hate us. He wants us close to Him. And it's our own fault if we stay out in the cold, because God has created a way to welcome us back in.

Drop your weapons and come inside for the party.

———————

You are not a God who takes pleasure in evil; with you the wicked cannot dwell. The arrogant cannot stand in your presence; you hate all who do wrong.

PSALM 5:4–5

24

7

Inside the Palace

Outside the king's palace, you wake to see hanging on the gate the same sign that your commander had shot up during the night: WELCOME. LEAVE YOUR WEAPONS OUTSIDE. ROYAL FEAST AT MIDNIGHT. COME EARLY. It's freshly painted, the bullet holes gone. You spook when you see the king walking around the palace gardens with tools in hand. *The king himself fixed the sign.*

Suddenly you understand that the rebels are wrong. You slip off your firearms and ammo belt and bolt through the gate toward the king.

You had been told that dobermans and land mines would mutilate anyone inside the king's gate, but when you reach the king you realize you haven't been blown apart. "The sign—" you gasp, out of breath. "It's true, isn't it?"

"It is," the king replies. "Welcome. I've been waiting for you."

📖 **Read Colossians 1:21–23. How can we stop being rebels against God?**

You probably don't try hard to be buddies with your enemies. But that's exactly what God has done. Even though the human race wasn't interested in a truce, God opened a gate back to himself through Christ (Romans 5:8).

We've all made ourselves God's enemies, deserving death—total separation from God—for our sins (Romans 6:23). Yet God sent His Son, Jesus, to suffer our punishment. He's the welcome sign, your invitation to enter the palace of King God, and the gate back to God. You accept God's invitation by putting down your weapons, by admitting to Him your sinfulness and need for His forgiveness: "God, you're King of the Universe. I've rebelled against you by what I think, say, and do. My rebellion deserves death, but I know now that Christ died in my place."

That's how you bolt through the gate back to the King. That's the beginning of being a Christian.

When you accept Christ's death for you, God says you're welcome back in His palace as His son or daughter. You've been "reconciled," made friends again. He promises you the never-ending royal feast of heaven (John 5:24), a feast you can start on now by enjoying friendship with God and other believers here on earth.

The sign is true. It's up to you to respond. Are you still a rebel, or have you gone through the gate and become a child of the King?

———————

Once you were alienated from God and were enemies in your minds because of your evil behavior. But now he has reconciled you by Christ's physical body through death to present you holy in his sight . . .

COLOSSIANS 1:21–22A

8

The Ultimate Coach

With bat in hand, the coach flipped a baseball into the air and hammered it toward right field. Rob back-pedaled as fast as he could, but the ball still soared over his head and hit the ground before he reached it.

"GET IN HERE!" Coach bellowed, and Rob ran to home plate. "Who's going to get the ball if you don't, Robby?" Coach said sarcastically.

"No one, sir."

"Give me fifty. NOW!" Rob did fifty push-ups and ran back to right field. But then he missed a short pop-up, and a grounder skipped between his legs. It was a bad afternoon—lots of mistakes, lots of push-ups.

📝 **Read Ephesians 4:17–24. How does God change us for the better?**

Every Christian starts out like a baseball player who needs to learn the basic skills of the game. Not one of us is perfect.

In fact, we need a *lot* of help. Without Christ, we have our caps pulled over our eyes. We stumble around unable to determine right from wrong—and we can't follow the ball of God's truth. We're out of shape—pretty much dead—and we've forgotten the sensation of God's life. We don't understand the game of life—we believe the lie that evil will make us outrageously happy, and we crave worse and worse things more and more.

God looks at us and says things have to change. When we come to Christ we put off evil thoughts and actions like a grimy, sweaty uniform, and put on a new life created by God. That process starts when we become Christians, and keeps on until we reach heaven.

And here's the good news: God isn't a nasty coach waiting for you to mess up so He can explode at you, kick you off the team, or punish you with push-ups while He looks on with a cruel grin. He works by changing the way you think and feel.

He gently remakes you from the inside out, teaching you that in the long run sin never makes you, Him, or the rest of the world happy. Then you can respond to God out of love, not fear.

God respects you. He doesn't scream at you. He knows He built you a brain.

You were taught . . . to be made new in the attitude of your minds, and to put on the new self, created to be like God in true righteousness and holiness.

EPHESIANS 4:22–24

9

You Belong on the Bomb Squad

When the bus pulled to a stop in the tiny Texas-Mexico border town, Tiffany flew down the steps feeling like a cartoon superhero. She and twenty other super-charged junior highers were about to battle the forces of darkness—handing out Bibles and building houses as a way of demonstrating God's love.

Tiffany felt like a hero—that is, until her feet hit the ground. Then she didn't feel heroic at all. She wore jeans instead of blue tights and a T-shirt instead of a cape; her heart pounded with panic, and she remembered she couldn't speak Spanish. One whiff reminded her she was far from home. What was she thinking when she signed up for *this*?

☑ **Read Ephesians 2:8–10. What does God plan for us as believers once we've accepted His "grace"—forgiveness through Christ?**

Sinning isn't like flicking a firecracker that pops harmlessly on the ground. It's more like tossing a match at a truckload of dynamite, then sticking around to watch. You don't walk away in one piece. Some explosions—selfishness, jealousy, greed, anger—shred hearts one at a time. Other blasts—adultery, abuse, abortion, war, hunger—maim whole crowds.

29

Trusting in Christ's death for you makes you God's son or daughter. You don't deserve God's forgiveness—that's what the Bible calls "grace." But God doesn't plan for His children to just lounge around the palace.

Don't worry. God doesn't expect you to be a super-hero.

He wants you on the bomb squad.

Your first mission is to let God help you love the people you see every day, so you defuse the explosives in your own life. Then you can start to befriend kids struggling at school, to help older people in your neighborhood, teach kids at church, serve in the inner city, or go on a short-term mission trip. God will use you to prevent explosions and repair the damage sin has done to the world, by doing the things God plans for you as a Christian.

You don't need special orders from headquarters. All believers are on the bomb squad. Just look around and get started. The bombs are everywhere.

For we are God's workmanship, created in Christ Jesus to do good works, which God prepared in advance for us to do.

EPHESIANS 2:10

10

He Has Plans for You

"Mom, I'd like to go camping with Allison's youth group," Kristi said quietly. "It's right after school gets out. It's not very much money, and a bunch of people are going."

"You want to sign up for *what*?" Kristi's mom mocked. "Let me see that." She grabbed the brochure. "Did you see how far they hike—and in the mountains?"

"I know," Kristi pleaded. "I know it will be hard, but I want to try."

"Get that idea out of your fat little head," her mom spat. "You'd die out there. Who will roll your body back?" When her mom finished laughing she spat some more. "You know, this is just another one of your stupid ideas. You're useless. Maybe collapsing out in the woods would prove that to you. You'll *never* amount to anything."

It's awful to be declared worthless and tossed away. After all, even trash gets recycled. Even garbage has a future.

▶ **Read Proverbs 3:1–6. What does the future hold for those who know God?**

If you have no hope, you'll seek relief however you can find it—even in ways that bury you alive, like pushing away people who love you or isolating yourself in a world between the ear pads of your headphones. You'll seek revenge—to show everyone how bad you can be.

When God's people were at their lowest low—they had been taken as prisoners to a faraway land—God gave hope to people who felt like forgotten trash. Here's what He said: " 'I know the plans I have for you,' declares the Lord, 'plans to prosper and not to harm you, plans to give you a hope and a future' " (Jeremiah 29:11). God doesn't promise to make believers bazillionaires, or to snatch them from sickness or hardship. Yet even when faith in God leads to tough times (Hebrews 11:35b—40), a future with God is worth anticipating.

Your bright future starts now if you live close to Him. But you can't sit waiting for God to fix life. It's when you "keep God's commands" and "trust in the Lord" and "in all your ways acknowledge him" that God can "make your paths straight."

Trust in the Lord *with all your heart and lean not on your own understanding; in all your ways acknowledge him, and he will make your paths straight.*

Proverbs 3:5—6

11

No Lie

Mitch rounded the corner just as Caveman's fist pounded Steve's stomach. Mitch tried to duck back, but Caveman—a gargantuan kid who spoke little and showered less—hoisted Mitch a foot off the ground and shoved him against a wall.

"Didn't see nuthin', did ya?" Caveman grunted. Mitch's feet tap-danced against the wall. Mitch shook his head *no*. "Tell anyone, you look like Stevie. Understand?" Steve was doubled over and holding his stomach, wheezing and whimpering. Mitch nodded his head *yes*.

Later a teacher stopped Mitch to ask if he knew who hurt Steve. Mitch said he didn't and walked off to blend in with a crowd of students.

If God wanted to, He could really mess up our minds. He could be a knuckle-breaking brute, scaring us into believing *His* version of the story, no matter what we had seen with our own eyes. Or He could be a different kind of liar—a deceiving charmer, winning our love one moment only to drop us with a *splat* the next. Because He's bigger and smarter than any of us, God could outmaneuver, out-argue, and outwit us, making us believe lies. But He doesn't.

Read Isaiah 45:18–19. How do you know that God tells the truth?

We don't always want the truth. We believe lies—and tell them—to keep life pleasant.

Unlike us, God swears to be honest in everything He says. He makes some huge promises: (1) He speaks openly, for everyone to hear; (2) He doesn't tease—when He tells His people ("Jacob's descendants") that they can seek Him and know Him, He means it; (3) He speaks not just truth but *the* truth; and (4) He—and no one else—knows perfectly what is right.

Big promises. But we can be sure they're not big lies. We would be stupid to trust what God says if He were out busting knuckles or breaking hearts. He's not. His honest words are backed by honest actions.

God's ultimate promise is to be God for everyone who trusts Him: "There is no God apart from me, a righteous God and a Savior" (verse 21).

And when God sent Jesus, He gave us the ultimate proof that He means what He says.

"I am the LORD, and there is no other. I have not spoken in secret, from somewhere in a land of darkness; I have not said to Jacob's descendants, 'Seek me in vain.' I, the LORD, speak the truth; I declare what is right."

ISAIAH 45:18B–19

PART 2

Hangin' on the VINE

12

Bewildered No More

This is so stupid. While all of Lisa's friends romped at the beach, she rotted in church.

Lisa's mom had separated from her dad three years ago because he drank and beat up the family, and the divorce was finalized a few months back. About the time of the divorce, Lisa's mom started going to church. She said she had found God and He was putting her life back together.

Whoopee for her, Lisa thought. *But why drag me here? I've got a life. Besides, God's like Dad. Useless.*

Lisa's friends got her into trouble sometimes, but at least they stuck together. Lisa had never seen God, but she'd seen her friends. They were dependable. She wasn't so sure about God.

Read John 4:19–26. (The passage picks up in the middle of a conversation between Jesus and a woman drawing water at a well.) How do we know what God is like?

Lisa isn't the only one confused about God. Teachers may argue that God is a figment of your imagination, the product of a childish wish. A non-Christian friend may admit Jesus was pretty cool, but to her the cross she wears is just jewelry—something that dangles from her ear. Our culture pictures God as the big Kahuna, the boss upstairs, a merciless judge, a deaf old duffer.

Confusion about God isn't new, either. A long time ago Jesus told the woman at the well that she needed to get her facts straight. When she tried to pull Him into an argument about the best spot to worship God, Jesus told her she was missing the point. Ceremonies and services and holy places are crusty, dusty religion if you don't "worship in spirit and truth," if your heart doesn't respond to God because you know who you worship and why.

Jesus revealed to the woman that He wasn't merely a prophet, someone who speaks *on behalf* of God, but the "Messiah," God as a human, who came to speak *for himself* with the human race—and, even more than that, to save it from destroying itself.

Jesus came because God wanted to prove His power and trustworthiness to us. He wants us to understand clearly what He is like (John 1:14; Colossians 1:15).

He wants us to see that He's the One to listen to.

———————

The woman said, "I know that Messiah" (called Christ) "is coming. When he comes, he will explain everything to us." Then Jesus declared, "I who speak to you am he."

JOHN 4:25–26

13
Twinkies for Lunch

You woke when the waves sloshing against the shore tickled your toes. You remembered the storm, and being tossed overboard, but that's it. The fog in your brain starts to clear, and you realize you're on a deserted tropical island. *Panic!* You wonder whether you'll shrivel up from starvation, or be mauled by wild animals.

Then you see it, a few yards up the beach: a boxcar-size crate of Twinkies.

"There is a God!" you shout. Sure, you're still shipwrecked, but you're the sole owner of an unlimited supply of your favorite food. You tan on the beach for the next day or two waiting to be rescued, humming reggae tunes and tossing down Twinkies. But when the rescue doesn't show, you discover something. You can't live on Twinkies alone. Better food, you figure, is behind you in the jungle.

📖 **Read John 6:30–40. What does Jesus say is the one thing that will sustain you for life?**

Chowing down one or two—well, maybe three or four—Twinkies at a time is a delectable snack. But they're not something you could eat meal after meal. You need real food.

A few verses before this passage, Jesus had fed five thousand people with a few loaves and fish. Some in the crowd claimed they would believe in Him if He could produce another sign—like burgers and fries raining from heaven. Jesus knew that all they wanted was to satisfy their physical hunger. So He taught them about spiritual hunger.

Jesus said that they needed more than the first convenient crate of Twinkies. If the crowd would just look around, they would see a limitless feast awaiting them in the jungle. Jesus declared, "I am the bread of life." He's not a snack. He's the feast of life in the jungle. He alone can permanently satisfy people's deepest hunger and thirst.

Jesus wasn't encouraging cannibalism. His words cranked the crowd's heads so they would look into the jungle. Jesus didn't just want to treat the crowd to lunch, He wanted to give them eternal life. But for them to accept His gift of eternal life, they needed to want more than a meal. They needed to want Him.

Then Jesus declared, "I am the bread of life. He who comes to me will never go hungry, and he who believes in me will never be thirsty."

JOHN 6:35

14

Give Me the Light

Until the weather sirens blasted him awake, Caleb hadn't noticed the rain knuckling the roof or the wet wind tearing at the curtains on his open bedroom window. The storm had knocked the power out, so he bumped through the dark to his parents' room. His older sister was holding his sobbing younger sister. Socks landed at his feet as his dad ransacked a dresser drawer to find a flashlight.

Just as Caleb's mom shooed everyone downstairs to shelter, lightning exploded a tree in the backyard. Even Caleb's dad bolted down the stairs—minus a flashlight to light the way or a radio to tell them what was going on. All the family could do was huddle in the dark basement and wonder what more the storm could bring.

📭 **Read John 8:12. How could Jesus be the "Light of the World"?**

On a stormy night with no lights you could bash your way around your house or apartment. You could cope. But if the lights stayed off and the storm kept on, your life would be scary and confining. You would wish for real sight.

Of course, after living in the dark for a time your eyes would adjust to the lack of light. You would get

41

along better than before. But when the lights came back on you would realize how little you could actually see.

Jesus came to shine into a world covered in spiritual darkness (John 1:4–5). Like a cloud, sin blocks out God's light. In its shadows wrong looks right. Good seems bad. The cloud spins off tornadoes and lightning and hail that spew destruction. But Christ lights up the world—His life shows the difference between right and wrong. And the closer you stick to Him, the better you see. He shines His light so you don't get lost in the dark.

After a while you might get used to the lack of light in your world. You start to think you can see pretty well. But when Jesus shows up, you realize that the shapes you saw in the darkness weren't what you thought they were. The light is the place to be. In the light every move doesn't result in a bump and bruise.

"I am the light of the world. Whoever follows me will never walk in darkness, but will have the light of life."

JOHN 8:12

15

Not That Dumb

Jill smelled trouble burning as soon as she walked in the door. As she tiptoed toward her bedroom her mom stopped her short. She held out a small plastic bag and asked Jill what was in it.

"It's parsley," Jill shrugged. "I chew it for my breath. All the kids do. It just dried out."

Her mom wasn't *that* stupid. "Don't play games, Jill. It's not dried parsley. It's pot. What are you doing with drugs in your backpack?"

"You were in my backpack? You have no right to go through my things."

"I was looking for the makeup you borrowed and didn't return. Jill, I can't believe you'd do this. I'm too angry to talk now. You go to your room until your dad gets home."

Jill exploded. "I'll go where I want to! You can't tell me what to do."

▶ **Read John 8:21–30. What did Jesus mean when He said "I am from above"?**

Members of the Flat Earth Society want you to believe—*surprise*—that the earth is flat. From observations you make in everyday life, it's tough to disagree with them. One glance outside should cause you to say, "Yup. Flat like a pancake."

But as soon as you get a bigger view—like the pictures of the earth astronauts take from space—you're forced to say, "Nope. Round like a ball."

A teen doing drugs doesn't want to admit that her parents or teachers or doctors have a better, bigger view of the danger of using drugs than she does. No one likes to be criticized, questioned, or condemned.

But we have to admit that we don't have the ultimate understanding of ourselves and our world. It's God who has the big picture: a view of all people and all events for all time.

Jesus said His teaching wasn't something He made up on His own. He spoke as God's Son, who came "from above," from the Father in heaven. He repeated what He heard from His Father. He warned us for our own good, so we could go back with Him to heaven (John 14:2–4).

Confusing? The crowds around Jesus thought so. But the point is that Jesus didn't speak as an ordinary human. He saw more than us. And He knows more than us.

"You are from below; I am from above. You are of this world; I am not of this world. I told you that you would die in your sins; if you do not believe that I am the one I claim to be, you will indeed die in your sins."

JOHN 8:23–24

16

Pink Bunny Sheets

You stroll to school wrapped in the only bed sheets left in the linen closet—your little sister's pink bunny sheets. You would have preferred plain white, but no matter. *People will still recognize me*, you reassure yourself. You step into traffic, protected only by a raised hand, and tires screech as cars skid to a stop. You raise your hand again to bless a neighbor's poodle.

When you get to school you don't take your seat. Instead you walk to the front of homeroom and command the class to be silent. "I have an announcement," you say. They stop to listen only because you look so wacko. "I will be running class from now on. You see, I am God."

You hear the class still snorting with laughter as your teacher escorts you to the principal.

☛ **Read John 8:48–59. Why did the crowd want to kill Jesus?**

If you told all your friends that you were God they would offer you a ride to a rubber room—once they stopped laughing, that is.

To many people it was just as preposterous when *Jesus* announced He was God. He was their neighbor, the ordinary son of a carpenter (John 6:42).

The crowd's reaction to Jesus seems strange to us.

45

He says "before Abraham was born, I am!" and they schedule a rock concert—and plan to use Jesus' brains as bongos. What could Jesus have possibly said that got them mad enough to kill Him?

Whenever Jesus used the phrase "I am _____" ("the Messiah," "the Bread of Life," and so on), He echoed the name God had given himself in the Old Testament, "I AM WHO I AM" (Exodus 3:14), a name so revered that the Jews didn't dare speak it aloud. For a man to claim that name for himself was a crime deserving death, according to Jewish law. In this passage Jesus' simple "I am" was a blunt claim to be the Eternal One, the God who existed before time began.

Some people say Jesus was merely a good man, a respected teacher like Confucius or Thomas Jefferson. But other great teachers didn't claim to be God. Jesus did. He knew what He meant. The crowd sure knew what He meant. And Jesus was willing to die for what He said.

"I tell you the truth," Jesus answered, "before Abraham was born, I am!" At this, they picked up stones to stone him, but Jesus hid himself, slipping away from the temple grounds.

JOHN 8:58–59

17

He Treats You Right

Four-year-old Marty peeked one eye around the chips and dips on the aisle end. *Not here.* He looked around another corner. *Not there.*

Lost in a cavernous supermarket filled with strangers, Marty pulled the strings on his jacket hood tight so that the hood hid his crying eyes and quivering lip. He shook with lostness. He howled with misery. He shrieked with terror. He'd lost his mommy.

He ran down aisle after aisle, farther from his mom. His mom, though, was already searching for him. Eventually, she caught up to him and picked Marty up, holding him tight. Marty buried his face in her hugs. "I'm here, Marty," she whispered. "It's okay. Mommy's here."

▶ **Read John 10:1–11. How do you recognize Jesus' voice?**

If a watchdog is well trained, it's suspicious of any stranger who comes near the house it protects. Nothing distracts it—throwing biscuits, cooing "Here, doggie, doggie" in your nicest voice, yelling "SHUT UP YOU DUMB DOG" while waving your arms like a wild man. A good dog can't be tricked. If you're not the dog's master, it won't be your friend.

A little child loves his mom's voice, and a watchdog

jumps when it hears its owner. As believers—like sheep—we learn to recognize our Shepherd's voice.

Sheep know their shepherd treats them right. He gives each a name. He provides for their needs—food during the day, shelter at night. The shepherd stands at the gate of the pen to check the sheep one by one, soothing wounds and providing security. The sheep know their shepherd's unique call, and scatter at anyone else's voice.

By experiencing the shepherd's kindness the sheep know that their shepherd isn't like others who sneak into the pen and hurt them. The shepherd's one concern is the good of those in his care.

Once you know that Jesus' main concern is to lead you into the best life God has in mind for you, then you won't be fooled by violent or stealthy voices that want to turn you into lamb chop. You know they don't sound like Jesus. Jesus' voice is kind. Jesus is your Good Shepherd.

The thief comes only to steal and kill and destroy; I have come that they may have life, and have it to the full. I am the good shepherd. The good shepherd lays down his life for the sheep."

JOHN 10:10–11

18
Don't They Get It?

Sweat beaded on Scott's lip. He looked left. He looked right. Just like last time—they were coming at him from all directions. Suddenly a guy built like a walk-in freezer flew through the air and tackled him.

Scott screamed, woke up, and sat up in bed. This time it was only a dream.

Next time he would think twice about busting the curve on a biology test.

Sometimes doing the right thing makes other people mad.

✏ Read John 10:31–39. What would you do if people kept chasing you with rocks?

It was the same thing all over again. The religious leaders wanted to kill Jesus, this time because He called himself "the Son of God." Jesus didn't mean God had given birth to Him. For Jesus to call himself "the Son of God" meant (1) that Jesus was God, and (2) that Jesus had a unique relationship with the Father. They were separate, yet one (10:30, 38).

Jesus didn't lie down and let His critics pelt Him. He knew He was right—that He did what pleased God and that His critics didn't. Jesus tried to persuade them by using Scripture. If they could accept that God

49

honored mere human rulers with the title "gods" or "sons of the Most High" (Psalm 82:6), then His claim to be the Son of God was no crime. He was, after all, God's special representative to the world.

And He offered His life as proof: *The works I do— healing disease, casting out demons, calming storms, feeding multitudes, raising the dead—show that what I say is true. The miracles I do are what my Father does. I am who I claim to be.*

Jesus' claims and the good He did go hand in hand. His actions alone are proof enough to believe, even if you don't believe His words.

So?

Jesus wants you to be sure about one thing. He can't make it any clearer without slapping it in your face: *When you look at me, you're looking at God. If you reject me, you reject God. If you don't follow me, don't claim that you're God's child.*

Believe me, Jesus argued. Some didn't. *You can't kill me for doing what's right.* One day they would.

"Why then do you accuse me of blasphemy because I said, 'I am God's Son'? Do not believe me unless I do what my Father does. But if I do it, even though you do not believe me, believe the miracles, that you may learn and understand that the Father is in me, and I in the Father."

JOHN 10:36b–38

19

After the Funeral

Until she got cancer, Jamie's grandma lived two thousand miles away in Florida. When Jamie's parents called a family meeting to decide whether Grandma should come to live with them, Jamie voted yes. Her parents said they wanted Grandma to die at home, with family surrounding her.

That sounded great a year ago.

Now it hurt. Jamie hardly knew her grandma before she moved in. If Grandma had died halfway across the country it wouldn't have mattered much. Jamie would have missed Grandma at Christmas and birthdays, but that was about it. Now Jamie knew her. Now she missed her. Jamie cried herself to sleep after the funeral. Her parents said they would see Grandma again someday. That sounded like a fairy tale.

☑️ **Read John 11:17–26. What happens to believers when they die? Why?**

Time-warp yourself sixty or seventy years into the future. You're at a funeral, but no one notices you're there. The old photos of the deceased in the back of the church look familiar, like pictures of a long-lost childhood friend. To take your mind off the organ music warbling in the background, you line up to view the body.

When you look into the casket, you see *you*—drained of life, caked in makeup, laid out in your best clothes. All around you, family and friends are sobbing.

If you could be a guest at your own funeral, what would you say?

For Christians, saying "we'll see Grandma in heaven" isn't an all-sugar treat we gulp down at funerals to make ourselves feel better. Death is a consequence of sin (Romans 6:23), but Jesus took the punishment for sin for all who believe in Him. Believers die physically, but death can't keep us down. Jesus is the Resurrection and the Life, and what Jesus did for Lazarus temporarily—check out verses 38 through 44—He will do for us permanently (John 3:16).

"I know you miss me," you would say if you could speak. "But don't cry forever. I followed Jesus. I'll be in heaven. I hope you'll be there, too."

Jesus said to her, "I am the resurrection and the life.
He who believes in me will live,
even though he dies."

JOHN 11:25

20
Stinky Feet

"Look out!" someone yelled at the team's star batter. "Willie's behind you!"

Too late. Willie lay on the ground wondering what planet he was on, walloped in the forehead by a wild warm-up swing. The bench emptied and everyone crowded around the Panthers' batboy.

"You weren't practicing where you were supposed to!" Willie's older brother yelled at Slugger.

"So?" Slugger shrugged and glanced at Willie still moaning on the ground. "Big deal. He's okay. Don't worry about it." He kicked at Willie. "Hey, kid. Get me some water."

☛ **Read John 13:1–5, 12–15. Why did Jesus wash His disciples' feet?**

Jesus picked a strange way to show strength. Politicians, for example, often stay on top by spewing lies and digging up muck. Gangs show who's boss by tagging turf and busting bodies. Some teachers keep control with threats of detention, suspension, and expulsion. It's hard to imagine politicians complimenting their enemies or gangs hugging their rivals. It's even hard to find teachers who inspire respect instead of provoking fear.

Jesus is the ultimate Teacher. All things are under His power—He's the Master of the universe. But you wouldn't have known it when He washed His disciples' feet. Rather than demanding honor and cursing anyone who didn't bow to His whims, Jesus did the job of the lowest household servant. He took off His shirt, wrapped a towel around himself, then unlaced the sandals and washed the feet of a dozen burly men who had spent the day tramping along dirt roads. Sweat, dust, and leather—imagine how bad it reeked. It would be better to chase balls and fetch water.

Jesus' disciples should have washed *His* feet.

He washed theirs.

He used His power not to knock His disciples down but to lift them up.

To us Jesus sometimes looks like a batboy. But don't mistake Jesus' servanthood for weakness or stupidity. He's really the King.

"You call me 'Teacher' and 'Lord,' and rightly so, for that is what I am. Now that I, your Lord and Teacher, have washed your feet, you also should wash one another's feet."

JOHN 13:13–14

21

Here Kitty, Kitty

Blistered from scurrying down miles of backcountry gravel roads, your paws hurt. What a lousy vacation this turned out to be! You're a thousand miles from home, and after a week you've seen no trace of your owners, whom you misplaced when you ditched your kitty carrier to search for mice. The tasty feast never happened. Definitely bad judgment.

You can't ask directions. No one understands your lonely *meow*. No one knows who you are or where you belong. Maybe if you keep searching you'll find your owners again.

Fat chance.

Stories of pets sniffing their way home across thousands of miles make for tear-jerker movies and quaint urban legends. But face facts: The only kitty that gets home is the one whose owner tracks it down and carries it back.

📝 **Read John 14:1–7. Where does Jesus plan to take His followers someday?**

As human beings we're lost—but not because our Owner decided He was tired of caring for us. We weren't flung out of a moving car in the middle of nowhere, or stuck in a bag and sunk to the bottom of a lake. We wandered away from God (Isaiah 53:6). And we're a long ways away.

Asking people how to get back home isn't much help. They're lost too. *Look for god inside yourself*, they say. *Work hard to be good enough for god. Trust cold concrete data and nothing else. Accept fate. Make up your own beliefs. Look to spirits and stars. Pummel your body to perfection. Get rid of desire—care about nothing.*

Human thought can't lead you through life to an eternity of paradise with God. Its destinations are confused. Its routes are dead ends.

Jesus knows where to take you and how to get there. He's tracked you down. He says, "I am the way and the truth and the life. Want to come home?" Only Jesus is the Way—He died for you and opened the gate back to God. Only Jesus is the Truth—He gives a perfect picture of God. Only Jesus is the Life—He conquers death so you can live eternally.

He's the one road back to where you belong.

Jesus answered, "I am the way and the truth and the life. No one comes to the Father except through me."

JOHN 14:6

22
Resolutions

The clock struck midnight. Everyone cheered and smooched, but Katie faked a smile. She thought about the past year—*what a wreck!* She had spent most of the year in her room, grounded from the phone and the TV and from getting together with friends. She had fought so much with her mother that her dad threatened to send her to boarding school.

Katie was even more bummed because she knew that deep down it was her fault. Her own stubbornness caused the problems with her parents. She told them she wanted to make her own mistakes. She did. The mistakes hurt. So in the first few hours of the new year, Katie resolved to obey her parents even before they opened their mouths. She closed her eyes and made her promise. When she opened her eyes she smiled, convinced things would be better.

They weren't.

If happy thoughts and resolutions were enough to make us better people, then the world would already be a paradise. Well, at least fighting and nail biting would be extinct.

Jesus came to make it clear, however, that it wasn't human promises but a divine Person—Jesus himself—who would make us new people. It's through *Him* and everything He's done for us that we grow up spiritually.

Read John 15:4–5. What does it mean to "remain in" Christ?

Horticulture lesson: Fruit doesn't appear in a grocery store out of nowhere. It comes from fruit-bearing plants. It starts on a vine, tree, or bush.

Christ taught that He is the one True Vine. We are the branches. If we want to bear good fruit—if we want to mature spiritually—we have to "abide" or "remain in" or "stay connected" to Him.

Fruit won't grow on a branch that's not in contact with the vine. Our promises mean little. We break them. Trying on our own to be good—without Christ's help—gets us nowhere. We wear out. What matters is relying on God, through His promises, to forgive us, live in us, teach us, and encourage us—and to be close to us as we stay close to Him.

I am the vine; you are the branches. If a man remains in me and I in him, he will bear much fruit; apart from me you can do nothing.

JOHN 15:5

23

A Promise or a Threat?

It was a little like getting a fortune cookie written by Dad every morning for breakfast.

Whenever Ryan's father went on business trips he left a stack of dated envelopes on the kitchen table, each with a note inside for Ryan to read while he was gone.

Sometimes there were lists of things for Ryan to do. A few notes were warnings—like nudging Ryan to study ahead for an upcoming test. Once in a while an envelope contained money to treat the rest of the family to pizza or a movie.

The notes reminded Ryan that his dad cared about him. They also made it hard for Ryan to forget that his dad had high expectations of how he would act, even when his dad wasn't around.

☛ **Read Revelation 22:12–16. After Jesus ascended to heaven He appeared to His disciple John to reveal "what must soon take place" (Revelation 1:1). What did He promise?**

Three times in the last chapter of the Bible Jesus said that He would return to earth (22:7, 12, 20).

That's a threat. It's also a promise.

When your parents leave you home alone and you

59

do things you shouldn't, you might dupe them into thinking everything went swell—that you did your homework, that you didn't blast the stereo loud enough to rattle the dishes, or invite friends over when they said not to.

Jesus can't be fooled like that. That's the threat.

But the promise is that Jesus is coming to remake the world the way He wants it to be—with God on the throne, and no death or crying or pain (Revelation 21:1–5). He is the "Alpha and Omega" (the first and last letters of the Greek alphabet). He created the world and controls its destiny. Those who "wash their robes"— who accept forgiveness and new life in Christ—will spend eternity with God in paradise.

God sometimes feels far away. Yet through the Bible He's written us notes to read daily—warnings, things to do, words meant to remind us of His love and to encourage us to do what's right until He comes.

Do you believe His notes? Is He the One you listen to?

"Behold, I am coming soon! My reward is with me, and I will give to everyone according to what He has done. I am the Alpha and Omega, the First and the Last, the Beginning and the End."

REVELATION 22:12–13

PART 3

Livin'

under

HEAVEN

24

Is God a Wimp?

Tasha didn't mean to be nosy, but from what she could see there weren't many books in the locker across from hers, even though three people crammed their stuff into it. It seemed like the most popular locker in school. There was never a crowd, but someone was *always* there—before school, after school, between classes. The locker was a puzzle, but it didn't bother Tasha—except that sometimes she felt left out. Whatever was going on, she sure wasn't part of it.

Then one day she saw an argument at the locker. Faces tensed, pills spilled, a knife flashed. The dispute ended quietly, but that didn't calm Tasha. She felt unsafe. She felt guilty because now she knew why the locker was so busy. And most of all she was angry at the school. They must know what was going on. The people in charge were either stupid or they didn't care.

When you consider the ugliness of our world—sickness, hatred, divorce, abortion, starvation, genocide—it's easy to conclude that God is distant. Stupid. Uncaring. Powerless.

☑ **Read Isaiah 46:3–13. Is God a wimp?**

The Bible portrays God as all-knowing and all-powerful, big enough to direct the galaxies—yet near enough to spin every atom of His creation. He carries His people from the beginning of life until old age—He creates, carries, and rescues. He predicts the end while at the beginning. He will accomplish all His goals. No one compares to Him. He is God, and there is no other. God is in charge.

The world doesn't always look that way. God is Master of the universe, the Beginning and the End—but if He's so powerful and so loving, how can His world be so ugly?

Here's the catch: God intends the world to be a place of righteousness, where people accept His love and live together in peace the way He planned. Yet God gives people freedom, the chance to follow or disobey His commands.

God says that when everyone listens to Him and trusts His authority, life will be heavenly.

Unfortunately, not everyone agrees.

I am God, and there is no other; I am God, and there is none like me.

ISAIAH 46:9B

25

The Jester

The gloomy clouds gathering over the kingdom fit the sour mood that had afflicted the king's subjects since they had heard the rumor about a country with no king. In that imaginary country no one told the people what to do, or what not to do. People there, it was said, were exceedingly wise and happy, each having the freedom to do as he pleased.

The king's subjects supposed that their lives must be boring by comparison. Though they had been entirely pleased with the king's rule, they grumbled that their lives should belong to themselves, not to the king. Yet no one thought to do anything about their discontent until the king's jester made up a rhyme:

The king is bad
And you are sad
Of course he is to blame.
Just follow me
And you will see
Your lives won't be so tame.

The people decided that day to live as if they had no king, shutting out his provision and ignoring his commands.

▶ **Read Isaiah 14:12–14. What did the being described by Isaiah do wrong?**

A human being who rules a country with total control is called an "absolute monarch" or a "dictator." No human being has the right or the ability to handle that much power.

God does. God is no human being. He *is* ruler of all. He made everything and has complete authority over it (Psalm 24:1–2). That would be unbearable if God's love for us weren't perfect. God's total love, total knowledge, and total power make Him worthy of our total devotion.

But not everyone agrees. The Bible talks in a hazy way about the beginning of a rebellion against God. Satan, whom God had made the most beautiful of all created beings (Ezekiel 28:12–19), decided *he* should be in charge. He believed he was wiser than God.

Satan is the jester who puts our fears into words. He spends his time trying to persuade the world that *he*, not God, is the one worth listening to.

He's wrong.

You said in your heart, "I will ascend to heaven. I will raise my thrown above the stars of God . . . I will make myself like the Most High.

Isaiah 14:13–14

26

He Doesn't Wear
Red Tights

Luke pulled out a Mercedes Benz hood ornament strung on a long chain inside his shirt. "Cool, huh?!"

Toby was a little shocked. He was sure Luke hadn't found his latest fashion statement at an auto parts store.

"No big deal," Luke spouted. "That's why people have insurance. Besides, people who drive cars like that have plenty of money to fix them. Fifty or a hundred bucks is like buying bubble gum to them. You want to go get one?"

"My parents would kill me if—" Toby tried to protest.

Luke just rolled his eyes with an expression that said, *Don't be such a doorknob.* "No one's gonna find out."

📑 **Read Genesis 3:1–7. How did Satan make rebellion against God look good?**

The Garden of Eden apparently was the only place Satan wore a snakeskin suit to get human beings to listen to him. But he's still devious. He twists thoughts so that good seems bad and bad seems good.

In his chat with Eve ("the woman" in the passage), Satan questioned whether God had said anything at all about eating fruit or letting it hang. He wanted Eve to think that specifics about right and wrong didn't matter much, even to God. Satan and Eve both made God's rule tougher than God had. (Look at Genesis 2:16–17. God only forbade eating fruit from one tree.)

Then Satan told Eve the consequence she feared was really just a fib. She wouldn't die, even though God said she would. And finally Satan lured Eve in with one last morsel: The reason God laid down the law was to deprive her of something wonderful.

Satan's tactics haven't changed. The fright and flash of devil worship and heavy-metal album covers are just a diversion from his widespread, everyday deceit. His voice hisses all around us: *You can make up your own mind, run your own life. Nothing will happen. God just wants to rain on your party.*

Don't expect Satan to pounce at you from behind a corner, sporting red tights and a tail, shouting, *"Hey, you! Wanna sin?"*

Satan still slithers like a snake.

"You will not surely die," the serpent said to the woman.
GENESIS 3:4

27

The Art of
Self-Defense

Joel rammed the joystick. His weapons display blinked WEAPONS LOCKED ON ENEMY TARGET. He fired. Hah! Four choppers and eight tanks blown to microbits. MISSION ACCOMPLISHED. RETURN TO BASE. Nothing better than zinging around in a helicopter gunboat shooting rockets and laser-guided missiles.

When Joel's parents told him they were divorcing, he felt like he had been shot—except this was no video game. Joel tells himself and his friends that he's okay, but he spends most of his time alone, shooting up digital enemies. The rules are simple—kill or be killed. There's nothing to figure out. Vaporizing his enemy means he wins.

Joel hit a key to play again.

Read Luke 4:1–13. How do you defend yourself when you feel attacked?

It's easy to believe God when things go well. You're certain: *God is good. God is powerful. God is right. God loves me. God tells the truth.*

It's not so easy to believe when life explodes. That's when you wonder why people treat you rotten, why your family fights, why school is so hard. When you can't figure out why God doesn't fix it all, you're tempted to start thinking differently about Him: *He's evil. He's weak. He's mistaken. He doesn't care. He's trying to trick me.*

When circumstances grew tough for Jesus and He was tempted to stop believing and stop obeying His Father, He fought back with Scripture. Jesus countered Satan's statements point by point with verses from the Old Testament (from Deuteronomy 8:3, 6:16, and 6:13). Jesus applied Scripture to His life, and Satan fled.

You can't shoot laser missiles at your thoughts, or at your enemies. But God's words are your weapon (Ephesians 6:17). You build up your ammunition every time you study your Bible. You fire when you say, "Hey, brain. Don't listen to that lie. It's not true. God says. . . ."

That's the only way you'll win.

The devil said to him, "If you are the Son of God, tell this stone to become bread." Jesus answered, "It is written: 'Man does not live on bread alone.' "

LUKE 4:3–4

28
Stupid Rocks

You struggled to keep your footing on the steep stairs as the canoe perched on your shoulders tipped forward and back and side to side. Each step tested your balance and tortured your already-tired muscles. You'd paddled eighteen miles and portaged overland four more. But climbing Stairway Portage was the worst—one hundred yards straight up. Once you had the canoes at the top, you climbed down and up twice again with all your other gear.

When you and your friends finally collapsed in camp that night, everyone opened up their packs. What you found wasn't a week's worth of food and clothing.

Your packs were full of rocks. Large rocks. Many large rocks.

You'd been sacked. Your *supposed* friends at base camp had snuck in and filled your packs with rocks.

Read Matthew 11:28–30. What kind of load does Christ ask you to carry?

If the Christian life were a canoe trip you would still face ridiculous portages, strong head winds, and crazed mosquitoes that zoom up your nose. Obstacles and opposition are part of life no one can escape. Life is often a toil. Being a Christian doesn't mean someone else will paddle your canoe while you kick back and duff.

But as a Christian you won't find back-busting rocks in your backpack. The One who maps your trip and packs your load wouldn't do that to you. The burden Christ calls you to carry is light. His authority—His "Lordship"—over you is kind and fair (Psalm 145:17). His love for you never ceases (Lamentations 3:22). He knows exactly how much you can lift (1 Corinthians 10:13). And He's there to unburden you when the weight becomes too much (1 Peter 5:7).

Contrast Christ with jokers who load your bags with boulders—some to be funny, some to be mean. Either way, you carry stuff you don't need to—heavy expectations, bad maps, bug repellent that doesn't repel, and sunblock that doesn't block.

That's what happens when you let anyone but Jesus pack your sack and guide you through life.

———————

Come to me, all you who are weary and burdened, and I will give you rest. . . . For my yoke is easy and my burden is light.

MATTHEW 11:28, 30

29
In a Coffin

Jenna had hoped for a little more excitement when she passed around the photos from her two-week summer mission project. Her friends flipped quickly through the pictures. They looked bored when she shared the intense excitement of teaching kids about Christ. They weren't even interested in the story about her hanging upside down, thirty feet off the ground, on a ropes course where her group worked on team unity.

She felt like a reject at her own welcome-back party. After Jenna shut the door behind the last guest, she ran to her room and thought horrible thoughts about the trip. She wanted to throw away the pictures. She wished she could throw away the mission trip. She wondered if she still had any friends.

📝 **Read John 12:23–28. What did Jesus mean by falling into the ground and dying?**

When Jesus said we should "hate life" and "die" like kernels of wheat, He spoke harshly to make a point— as in "Don't have a cow" or "You eat like a pig." Jesus doesn't want us to kiss speeding trucks or to gulp poison together like cults do. To "hate your life" or "to die," Jesus explained, is to follow Him, to trust and obey Him in every situation of life, to let Him be Lord.

Obeying God can feel like you're dying, like you're being buried alive. Cheery thought.

The pain that can result from obeying God, though, is only half the story. After death comes life. A seed wrapped tight in a package on a shelf won't grow. Only when a seed is dropped into the ground does the soil's scratchiness and cold wetness force a plant to spring up.

At times even Jesus prayed, "God, I'd like to get out of here. I don't want to do this" (Matthew 26:39). Yet He always faced God's plan with anticipation—even the cross—because He saw past death to life on the other side.

In the midst of death God grows new life in you and in others. Suffering as a Christian—falling into the ground and dying—feels about as fun as lying trapped in a coffin. Remind yourself of one thing: God promises that you won't be in there forever. He'll come and lift you out.

"I tell you the truth, unless a kernel of wheat falls into the ground and dies, it remains only a single seed. But if it dies, it produces many seeds."

JOHN 12:24

30

Mutant Librarian's Daughters

Bad timing. You exit a store at the mall and right in your face is the school librarian. Earlier today you really made her nostrils smoke. Your latest little game is to tip your chair up on the back legs until she yells to put it down. Today you made her so furious she just about knocked you off your chair herself. And now there's nowhere to run—she's spotted you.

She's holding hands with some guy. *A husband? The monster's married?* And two girls are with them. *Daughters? She's reproduced?* You imagine her daughters as freaks bred to inflict pain on another generation of students. Then you blink. They're about your age, and actually pretty.

"Hi!" the monster waves. *Strange—she sounds friendly.* She introduces her family and then pulls you aside. She says she hopes she hasn't been too hard on you. She doesn't want you to get hurt, and she explains that the custodians are always after her for chairs breaking in the library.

As she walks away with her family, the library lady looks a little different to you. You had never noticed she was a human being.

Read 1 Timothy 2:1–2. How can you get along with people in authority?

God is King over all creation, and the Bible reveals how we should live under His Lordship. Still, we don't answer *only* to God. Often He places us under the authority of people—parents, teachers, police, employers, the government—who in some way have the power to punish evil and reward good (1 Peter 2:14). At other times God places people under *our* leadership. If everyone does his or her part, the world runs smoothly. God says plainly that He expects us to submit to the authorities over us (Romans 13:1).

Even so, submission—accepting and obeying authority—doesn't mean bagging your brain. You help leaders lead you when you're involved in their leadership. Start by praying that they will lead wisely (1 Timothy 2:2). At the right time tell them your point of view. Talking accomplishes more than being bitter and silent. And try to treat authorities as people, even if you're convinced they're not.

If you want leaders to be fair to you, you need to be fair to them.

I urge, then, first of all, that requests, prayers, intercession and thanksgiving be made for everyone—for kings and all those in authority. . . .

1 TIMOTHY 2:1–2A

31

Not Just on Mother's Day

With his mouth full of food, Matt outlined his afternoon plans. His mom glared at him coldly. "Aren't you forgetting something? Shouldn't we do something *I* want to do?"

"Why?" Matt asked and kept eating the lunch his mom had fixed.

"Here's a clue. It's Mother's Day today. You haven't even said 'Happy Mother's Day.' "

"Does that mean I can't go to a movie with my friends this afternoon?" Matt frowned.

Matt's mom gave up. "Fine. Forget about me. Go do what you want."

At supper Matt flung a small bag into his mom's lap. "Here's your present. Happy Mother's Day." His mom pulled the unwrapped present out of the bag. It was a black coffee mug that read, *I'M NOT FAT. I'M JUST SHORT FOR MY WEIGHT*.

Matt grinned at his mom. "Funny, huh?" She wasn't laughing. Matt backpedaled. "All the other ones said corny stuff like 'I love you.' What did you expect?"

▶ **Read Exodus 20:12. Why should you honor your parents?**

Honoring your parents means more than being nice to them one day a year. It means respecting, communicating with, and obeying them every day of the year. It means treating them the way you hope to be treated. Your parents deserve honor for giving you life and taking care of you.

You may not be impressed by the way they are parenting. You may even wish at times that they hadn't given you life. But God doesn't say to listen and obey only parents who you think deserve respect.

In the Old Testament God told His people that He would give them an incredible place to live, the "promised land." God told them that by obeying His commands they would live long and prosper in the land. His presence and care would be part of their daily lives. God promised specifically to bless those who trusted *Him* to guide them and shape them *through* their parents—even though parents aren't perfect. The same principle works now.

Believe that? Then trust God and honor your parents. Don't believe that? Then think about the flip side of the promise: Those who rebel against their parents will experience misery.

Honor your father and mother, so that you may live long in the land the Lord *your God is giving you.*

Exodus 20:12

32
Only If You Do What We Want

It seemed so cruel. But Lindsey wanted to fit in. And everyone was watching. So she agreed to the dare.

Andy was so slimy that Lindsey worried she might slip on the floor if she got too close. Still, she strolled over to the table where Andy sat alone studying calculus. She put her arms around his neck from behind and whispered in his ear: "Andy, I'd love it if you asked me to the dance on Friday night."

This was *truly* cruel. Lindsey had her arms around the nerdiest guy she had ever seen, and she was supposed to tell him this was a joke.

You pick the ending: (a) Lindsey jumps back, yells "Just kidding," and gains fourteen popular yet heartless friends; or (b) Andy turns to answer Lindsey, his hair smears grease across her face while he drools on her shoes, but Lindsey can't bear to break his heart. When they show up together at the dance, the school's social elite are not impressed.

Peer pressure usually isn't that obvious, but it might as well be. The crowd screams: "If *you do what we want*, then *we'll like you*."

✔️ **Read Galatians 1:10. Do you have to choose between friends and God?**

You don't *always* have to choose between popularity with people or popularity with God. Your friends may be great for you, supporting God's best choices and echoing God's voice. But it's a delusion to think that you never have to rebel against your peers to follow God.

Look at it this way: Peers deserve your friendship; they don't deserve to run your life.

God will be around long after your peers laugh at you, turn their backs on you, and walk away.

And—this is hard—pleasing God is infinitely more important than satisfying any peer. Jesus talked about peer fear when He said, "Do not be afraid of those who kill the body and after that can do no more. . . . Fear him who, after the killing of the body, has power to throw you into hell" (Luke 12:4–5).

Blunt. But true.

Am I now trying to win the approval of men, or of God? . . . If I were still trying to please men, I would not be a servant of Christ.

GALATIANS 1:10

33
Rulebusters

Within minutes after students heard that six of their favorite teachers would be laid off because of budget cuts, a plan had hatched. When the bell rang for third hour, students walked out of the school and planted themselves on the school's front lawn. The signs were unfurled. Students chanted, "NO MORE CUTS!"

When the students refused their principal's plea to return to class, they were suspended from school. The protesters fought with students who chose to stay in class. Parents whose kids were suspended complained that the punishment ignored students' rights to free speech. School administrators said the walk-out wasn't the best way to protest the cuts.

It's natural to want to retaliate when a person or group in authority does something we don't like. But is it right? When is it okay to disobey someone you're supposed to obey?

📝 **Read Acts 4:13–22. The "they" in verse 13 is a group of Jewish rulers. Why did Peter and John decide to disobey them?**

Disobeying authority isn't okay just because you don't feel like following the rules. Disobedience is an option only when God's commands are directly challenged—and only when all other methods fail. Peter tried reasoning before threatening disobedience, and *then* continued to preach because stopping would mean breaking God's clear command.

Most people—Christians included—agree that there are times when authorities are wrong and we should disobey them. Europeans hid Jews from the German Nazis. African Americans broke laws that mistreated them because of the color of their skin.

If you choose to break a rule, or engage in "civil disobedience," be willing to suffer the consequences. Daniel went to the lions' den for praying (Daniel 6). Shadrach, Meshach, and Abednego went to the furnace for refusing to bow to an idol (Daniel 3:16–18). Their stands against ungodly laws pointed out the wickedness of the laws and gave God the chance to display His power. Yet at the same time, their acceptance of punishment demonstrated respect for the authorities God had established (Romans 13:1–5).

If you're going to be a rulebuster, be ready to get busted.

But Peter and John replied, "Judge for yourselves whether it is right in God's sight to obey you rather than God. For we cannot help speaking about what we have seen and heard."

ACTS 4:19–20

34
Swine Diving

Who knows—maybe it's the sugar. Or maybe it's your expectation that sugar sends you into warp drive. Either way, you think you're funny. Hilarious. When you and sugar get together, you're a legend in your own mind.

At your friend's party you didn't stop after the chocolate chip cookie dough and two liters of Mountain Dew. You tried to set a personal best for the number of sugar packets consumed in one sitting. You were close to setting a record when someone yelled, "SWINE DIVE!" and the whole party headed upstairs.

Over and over you oh-so-elegantly leapt off a dresser and belly flopped on the bed across the room. But when you tipped the dresser and the bed crashed through the frame to the floor, your friend's dad sent you home. He said enough was enough. You were out of control.

You said you weren't to blame. It was the sugar.

🖝 **Read Proverbs 25:28. What good is self-control?**

Getting a sugar buzz sure isn't the only way to lose control of yourself. A guy who lets his friends tell him drugs are the ultimate trip has misplaced his brain. A girl who gets drunk and winds up in bed with a stranger loses her body—and maybe her health or her life. Letting your emotions or hormones run wild can destroy you. When you lose self-control, you're like an ancient city with broken-down walls. You have no protection. You have no power over who comes in or who goes out or what they do.

God respects you enough to make *you* ultimately responsible for yourself. He gives you parents and teachers and other authorities to instruct and shape you. But in the end, you answer to God for yourself. Having authority over yourself is God's gift that allows you to follow Him—not because you have to, but because you want to.

But you abuse God's gift whenever you surrender control of yourself to anything or anyone other than God. You might as well bind your hands, gag your mouth, and unplug your brain. If you don't control yourself, some other nasty thing will.

Like a city whose walls are broken down is a man who lacks self-control.

PROVERBS 25:28A

35

Lemmings and Lerts

Mama Lemming had it written big on the family calendar. *March 20*. First day of spring. Annual Lemming Migration.

Like all other good Lemmings, the family packed up their Lemmingmobile and headed toward the sea. Why to the sea? They didn't know. Everyone was going.

A minute out of the driveway the Lemming children grew impatient.

"Are we there yet?" Sister Lemming cried.

"How much farther?" Brother Lemming whined.

Papa Lemming found the expressway clogged with other Lemmingmobiles. "Oh, this is just great." Papa Lemming banged the steering wheel. "Now we'll never get there."

When the Lemmingmobile arrived at the sea, the Lemming family ran with all the other Lemmings into the sea, where the Lemming family—as well as all the other Lemmings—did *not* live happily ever after.

▶ **Read 1 Peter 5:8–11. Would you rather be a Lemming or a Lert?**

Lemmings are tough little ratlike rodents that live in northern Europe. When their colonies get too crowded, millions of lemmings leave their homes in

85

spectacular mass migrations. Sometimes they run into the sea. None of them bothers to find the answer to the one question that really matters: Is this a good idea?

No. Lemmings can't swim.

They don't intend to drown themselves. They're just looking for a nicer, less crowded place to live.

Lemmings are stupid. Lerts, on the other hand, ask smart questions.

If someone tries to lead a Lert along a line of living that looks like it lacks logic, a Lert likes to learn more: Who's leading this migration? Where are we going? Is it a good place to live? Lerts have learned to discern lies.

Unlike lemmings.

Don't be a lemming. Be alert.

Be self-controlled and alert. Your enemy the devil prowls around like a roaring lion looking for someone to devour.

1 PETER 5:8

PART 4

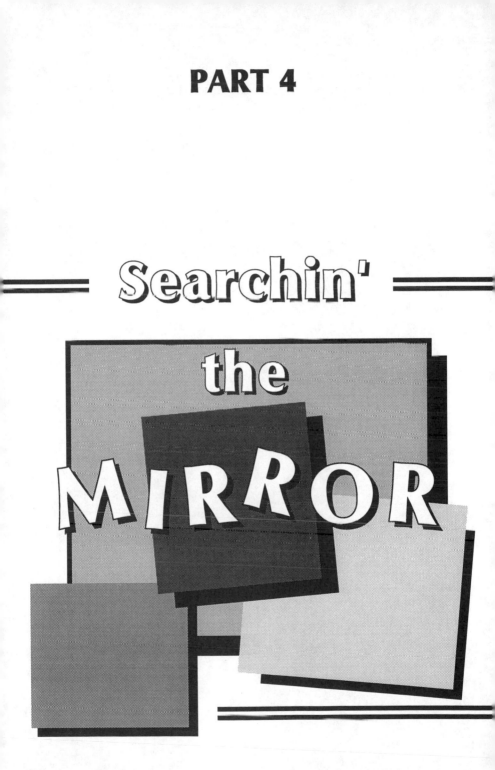

Searchin'
the
MIRROR

36

You're So Gullible

Matt saw the four-foot stuffed animal hanging in the carnival booth and knew that dog would win him Amber's love, at least for a day. All he had to do was shoot balloons with a BB gun. They weren't very far away. What could be easier?

"Everyone wins a prize!" the lady in the booth hollered. Matt unwadded a dollar bill and headed for the booth. His older brother knuckled him on the head.

"You're so gullible," Todd lectured. "It's a rip-off. See how you get three shots and then get a different gun? If you hit too many balloons you get a gun that doesn't shoot straight."

The lady running the game saw Todd whispering and pointing. "Hey, kid!" she yelled as they wandered to other games. "You chicken or something? If you're so good, get over here and show everyone."

You don't need a knuckle on your noggin to know that carnies don't run their games purely for your enjoyment. They want your money. They'll say whatever it takes to get you to play their games. But it's an uncheery thought to realize a carnival isn't the only place you're forced to sort truth from falsehood.

☑ Read Isaiah 59:1–11. What are people like when they don't listen to and obey God?

Truth is hard to find. Peers fib behind your back and then to your face. Sports stars inflate their images to sell you the goods. Musicians and media distort, deceive, and mislead. And if you hadn't noticed, even people who *want* to be honest with you make mistakes. There's one fact you can be sure of: People don't always tell the truth.

Without God changing our minds and words, people naturally follow the "ruler of the kingdom of the air" (Ephesians 2:2), who is the "father of lies" (John 8:44). Truth gets lost and life becomes a sticky spider's web, a shadowy darkness, a confusing carnival.

It would be nice to think you could accept as true anything that people tell you. But don't plunk down your money until you understand how the game is played.

Your lips have spoken lies, and your tongue mutters wicked things. No one calls for justice; no one pleads his case with integrity. They rely on empty arguments and speak lies. . . .

ISAIAH 59:3B–4A

37
Truth in a Toilet

Ten seconds ago the couple on-screen was goo-gooing into each others' eyes—sappy but harmless. All of a sudden they're kissing like a carwash during the scrub cycle. And it goes on and on. *Whew!* Your glasses fog. You didn't expect that in this movie.

Question: What do you do? Your choices: (a) Cover your eyes—but peek through your fingers; (b) Gawk and take notes; (c) Stomp out and never go to another movie; or (d) Ponder excuses for watching something you know you shouldn't.

No good answers.

Better question: Why are you at the movie? What are you looking for?

✔ Read Proverbs 2:1–11. How do you look for wisdom?

God's wisdom helps you "live in safety and be at ease, without fear of harm" (Proverbs 1:33). That sounds appealing—almost like the happiness and re-laxation you want from entertainment. Sometimes a movie or music provides a bit of what you're looking for. It says what you feel or expresses a truth about life. But it doesn't teach the knowledge of ultimate truth and reality that satisfies through and through. Only God's wisdom does.

Be honest. Lots of times you have to sit through a heap of bad to get a tiny bit of good. Trying to find wisdom in some places is like trying to find lost change in a toilet. It may be there, but it's not worth the dig.

Disgusting? You bet. But so is swishing through the swirl of waste you find in many TV shows, videos, tunes, concerts, magazines, books, comics, and computer games—not just the violence, bad language, and "adult situations," but the arrogance, sarcasm, and selfishness.

That isn't smart stuff. If you're looking for wisdom—for truth, reality—which leads to life, there's a better place to look.

Wisdom is treasure worth searching for. It's worth crying out for. And God is *the* place to get it. Don't bother looking for gold in an outhouse.

If you call out for insight and cry aloud for understanding, and if you look for it as for silver and search for it as for hidden treasure, then you will understand the fear of the LORD and find the knowledge of God. For the LORD gives wisdom. . . .

PROVERBS 2:3–6A

38

Your Hand Looks Dead

The last time Lauren raised her hand to ask a question in class, her science teacher said her hand resembled something dead he had dissected in college. Lauren cringed and slipped both hands under her desk. When everyone had stopped snorting at Mr. Cooper's remark, she peeked at her hands. She flip-flopped them in her lap. They looked plenty alive to her.

Mr. Cooper had been mean to Lauren ever since she missed school for a week because of the flu. Even though she tried hard, she hadn't caught up. She still was a test behind the rest of the class, and Mr. Cooper was treating her like an idiot.

Now she needed help again. She couldn't decide whether to brace herself for another rude remark or to keep her mouth shut and fail more assignments.

> **Read James 1:5. Does God make fun of you when you need His help?**

No one wants to look stupid or helpless. At school you would rather be bewildered than ask a teacher to explain the same point six times because you're still confused. At a party you would gladly cook all your CDs in an oven before you would admit you don't know how to dance. And around home you would sooner get your head pounded inside out than let your mom fight off a bully for you.

Admitting to yourself that you need help takes guts. Actually asking for it is even harder.

Once you get up the courage, what you don't need is to be made to feel like a bonehead—like a teacher who treats you as though you're stupid in order to make you work harder. Or like a parent who roughs you up to make you tough for the real world. Or like an employer who never lets employees forget who's boss.

When you can't tell right from wrong, good from bad, or truth from lies, God has the answers. But knowing He's the Ultimate Brain doesn't do you any good if you fear He'll mock you for needing help.

God doesn't laugh. He doesn't scold. He helps.

———————

If any of you lacks wisdom, he should ask God, who gives generously to all without finding fault, and it will be given to him.

JAMES 1:5

39
Just in Case

Ben knew that three months ago he could have asked God to show him how to survive Mrs. Weston's history class. He still wasn't sure, though, that he wanted to hear what God might have to say. So instead he whipped off a prayer at the end of his twelve-minute cram session the night before the final exam: "God, please make me do well on my history test tomorrow. I know you don't want me to flunk and develop poor self-esteem and spend my life sleeping in a gutter, so I trust you'll work on Mrs. Weston so I get an A. Thanks, God."

Praying made Ben sure God would come through for him.

Well, not totally sure.

By the time Ben started the test the next morning he had figured a foolproof way to an A, in case God didn't deliver. Not only did Ben have the encyclopedia of American history scribbled on his arm, but he had arranged to sit within easy eyeball range of the smartest kid in class. Between God, crib notes, and the son of Einstein—Ben had things covered.

▶ **Read James 1:6–8. What does it mean to be "double-minded"?**

If you constantly asked a friend for directions to her house—but always took your own route and then complained about getting lost—she would give up trying to tell you the way. Likewise, God knows that unless you're ready to listen and obey, showing you truth is useless.

God enthusiastically gives wisdom (verse 5) to anyone who asks. He expects you to trust His desire and ability to answer your request. He expects you to believe Him enough to act on the truth He shows you—to follow His directions, to walk His way, to do what He says.

Faith trusts. Doubt hatches backup plans. Double-mindedness picks and chooses. Part of you wants God's truth, part of you doesn't. Part of you wants to obey, part of you won't.

Don't assume it means your faith has to be perfect before God will answer you. No human being has perfect faith in God. What God wants to see is a faith that shouts, "I do believe. Help me believe more!" (Mark 9:24, *New Century Version*).

He who doubts is like a wave of the sea, blown and tossed by the wind. That man should not think he will receive anything from the LORD; he is a double-minded man, unstable in all he does.

JAMES 1:6–8

40
Wasted Waiting

Andrew inspected his list: Three months of clean socks and underwear. *Check.* Extra toothpaste. *Check.* Razor and shaving cream in case of an unexpected sprouting of facial hair. *Check, check.* Skip the deodorant. *Uncheck.* He'd be alone on his quest.

It would be a long wait. But he was ready.

Andrew set out early one Saturday morning at the beginning of summer vacation. He figured he should climb a mountain, but he lived in southern Minnesota. He did the best he could. He found a high spot in a nearby cornfield and set up camp. After he pitched his tent he carefully arranged cornstalks so they spelled "HELP!" when viewed from above.

Andrew wasn't waiting to be seen by a search plane. He was waiting for God—for a vision, a dream, a lightning bolt, a talking bush. He didn't care which. He wanted God to speak to him, to tell him the secret of life.

Don't worry. Finding God's truth isn't that hard.

📕 **Read 2 Timothy 3:14–17. Where do you go to hear God's voice?**

You can find truth in lots of places. God lets you learn from parents whose heads aren't empty and from grandparents and other older people whose lives have been full. He allows you to study history so you don't repeat people's mistakes, and to learn about science and the arts so you won't be stupid about your world. Sometimes you can learn from liars and lunatics.

But the Bible's truth is unique. It is inspired by God—"God-breathed"—so its truth is completely flawless. The Bible is a measurement for everything else that claims to be true—of a friend's words, a musician's lyrics, an author's ideas, a screenwriter's view of life. It corrects you when you're wrong and encourages you when you're right. God designed the Bible for you to read and apply with other believers so you can discover Him and understand yourself and your world.

Scripture is God's perfect, reliable, written word. It's the first test of who to listen to. It's the one place you can be sure you don't have to swish around in to find the truth.

All Scripture is God-breathed and is useful for teaching, rebuking, correcting and training in righteousness. . . .

2 TIMOTHY 3:16

41

But He Said He Loves Me

Wendy curled up on the living room couch to watch out the front window. She jumped at every passing car, and told herself that it was the snowy weather that had made her father late. But he was already two hours overdue, and a dark thought began to creep around in her head: *He's not coming.*

A few days earlier Wendy had received a letter from her biological father apologizing for running out on her and her mom ten years before. He promised to start spending time with his daughter. Wendy's mom warned her not to expect much, but Wendy's hopes ran wild. She was going to see her father again!

Now she sat staring out the window, blinking away her tears. *But he said he was sorry*, she told herself. *He said he loves me.*

She fell asleep waiting for her father, who never showed up.

📖 **Read 1 Corinthians 13:1–8. What does love have to do with truth?**

It's hard not to believe in a parent who wants to come back and make things right. Anytime *anyone* promises you something you really want, it's hard not to believe them.

But words aren't worth trusting if they aren't backed up by actions. From the Bible's point of view, truth is more than promises or bare facts or correct thoughts. Truth is something that is *lived*. Without love, words are worthless (1 John 4:18).

Truth without love is like poison in a popsicle: sweet but deadly.

Scripture is the first test of truth. Love is the second. People worth trusting aren't necessarily the ones who know the most, but the ones who combine knowledge with real-life love, the ones who look the most like the list in verses 4–7. People who love as God loves are the ones who have grasped truth.

You can't escape people whose brains are bigger than their hearts, but you can avoid being duped by them. You may need to pick a role model other than a parent. At times you'll need to study up on a point of view other than a teacher's. And sometimes you'll have to decide whether a friend is really a good friend.

If I have the gift of prophecy and can fathom all mysteries and all knowledge . . . but have not love, I am nothing.

1 Corinthians 13:2

42

It Makes a Poor Parachute

You settle into your seat. The flight attendant starts to rattle off the safety instructions. *Spare me*, you think. *Let's get this birdie in the air.* Just before she starts her speech, though, you interrupt and ask her why the plane is taking off late.

"Oh," she says, "we had an itsy bit of trouble getting a door shut. I think I fixed it." *THE DOOR?* your head explodes. *YOU HAD A PROBLEM WITH A DOOR? YOU THINK YOU FIXED IT?!* A few days earlier the same kind of plane dropped a door midflight and sixteen passengers were sucked out of the plane.

Your attention rivets on the flight attendant as she discusses sudden loss of cabin pressure and using your seat cushion as a flotation device. When she points to the plane's exits, you take it as a message from God. Better to deplane now than to skydive from 40,000 feet using your barf bag as a parachute.

► **Read Matthew 7:15–20. How do you spot a good person?**

When you board a plane you assume it's been tested, re-tested and re-re-tested by someone who knows what to look for. Unfortunately, no one tests mouths for truthfulness. And that's a problem: Anyone can fake truthfulness for a while. Anyone can seem loving from a distance.

So Jesus suggests a third test of truth: consistency. Jesus says people's lives are like trees. Watching what people produce over time shows their real nature. An athlete's approach to life may seem fast and cool until he charges people when they ask for autographs or sleeps around and dies of AIDS. Time makes it clear he's not what he seems to be. He may be a skillful player, but he's not someone you want to act, talk, think, or smell like.

You wouldn't get on a plane if you thought it would crash. Why take death-defying risks with who you listen to? A plane ride lasts a few hours. Who you listen to affects your whole life. You're safest with people who are probably already around you—youth leaders, Christian friends, parents—people who have *proven* that they speak truth and love you like God does.

By their fruit you will recognize them. Do people pick grapes from thornbushes, or figs from thistles? Likewise every good tree bears good fruit, but a bad tree bears bad fruit.

MATTHEW 7:16–17

43

When Truth Clashes

No one was surprised when Nina's older sister got pregnant. But Micki was shocked when she heard about the abortion.

"She did *what*?" Micki looked at Nina with sick eyes.

Nina stuck up for her sister. "I don't know what I'd do. But I sure wouldn't want to have a kid."

"How can you say that?" Micki blurted.

"I think you have to be there to know what you'd do." Nina looked at Micki like she was unbelievably stupid. "You just can't make that choice ahead of time."

"There's not much choice," Micki fought back. "Abortion is wrong."

☑ **Read 1 Peter 3:15–16. What can you do when what you believe clashes with what others believe?**

Most people look to something other than the Bible as their prime source of truth. They follow their feelings and do whatever feels good. They think technology has all the answers and decide God is unnecessary. They appoint their own brains as the absolute judge and decide for themselves what is right and true.

Then they criticize what Christians believe and how we live. Nonbelievers may point out our hypocrisy, selfish narrowness, and un-Christlike attitudes and actions.

Sometimes they're right. Because we're imperfect, our view of the world and of ourselves is imperfect. Criticism is a challenge to grow in what we know, to look at ourselves in the Bible's mirror and make sure we aren't a mess. We need to double-check that Christ is really in charge of our lives and that we understand Him and His Word correctly.

At other times the people who disagree with us are dead wrong. Then what?

Go ahead and explain as best you can what you believe and why. You may need to ask more mature Christians to help you know how to answer challenges, but it's okay to say "I don't know" and give an answer later.

God wants everyone to accept His truth. But *He* changes attitudes (2 Timothy 2:24–26). You don't. So don't explode. "A gentle answer turns away wrath, but a harsh word stirs up anger" (Proverbs 15:1).

But in your hearts set apart Christ as Lord. *Always be prepared to give an answer to everyone who asks you to give the reason for the hope that you have. But do this with gentleness and respect. . . .*

1 Peter 3:15

44
Stargazing

As she did every morning, Megan grabbed her favorite section of the newspaper out from under her dad's coffee mug. She couldn't start her day without reading her horoscope. Most days it read like the notes her mom tucked in her lunch box when she was little: *You'll have a happy day if you're nice to everyone.* But Megan had relied on her horoscope ever since the time it gave her the boost she needed to make the cheerleading squad.

Once a speaker told her youth group that horoscopes were demonic, but she kept reading them religiously. If they didn't make her foam at the mouth or encourage her to kill her family with an ax, she didn't see anything wrong with them.

Horoscopes—like Ouija boards, Magic-8 Balls, divination (foretelling future events), witchcraft, spells, psychics, tarot cards and palm readers, contacting the dead and channeling spirits—are attempting to tap into special supernatural power and knowledge that's hidden ("occult") from normal human senses (Deuteronomy 18:10–12).

▶ **Read Acts 19:13–20. What did the early believers do about their occult practices?**

You could make a lot of touchdowns if you hid the ball in a sack, snuck out of bounds, climbed through the stands, and dashed into the end zone. Trying to find a shortcut to truth might be just as tempting. It might even work. But it wouldn't be wise if the stands were full of enemy fans ready to tear your head off.

God has ruled certain sources of knowledge out of bounds, a danger zone. It's obvious why. The seven sons of Sceva discovered that the evil spirits sitting in the stands are nothing to fool around with. The early believers admitted to God that they had stepped way out of bounds, and then they trashed many millions of dollars of occult materials.

Some occult practices are scams. Others call on dangerous satanic spirits. What's really wrong with the occult, though, is that it seeks advice and help from God's archenemy, Satan. That's not just dangerous. It's pointless. God never hides truth from His friends.

A number who had practiced sorcery brought their scrolls together and burned them publicly. When they calculated the value of the scrolls, the total came to fifty thousand drachmas.

ACTS 19:19

45

Get Smart

Justin dreaded seventh-grade gym class—mostly using the locker room. After a few weeks, though, he decided the locker room wasn't so bad—especially when the guys talked about girls. The hot topics sizzled his ears. He knew what they said wasn't good, but it was funny—like their plans to drill a peephole into the girls' locker room.

Justin had never had a girlfriend, but he started talking as if he had a lot of experience. And he figured the other guys knew what they were talking about.

The talk didn't stop in the locker room. Instead of talking *about* girls, Justin started talking that way *to* girls. He joked about what he wanted to do with them. The more he talked, the more he wanted. And the more he wanted, the more he tried to get it.

📖 **Read 1 Kings 11:1–11. Why did Solomon lose his love for God?**

News programs are full of I'm-not-that-stupid stories: Flood victims who deliberately stayed too long perched on the housetop. Bodies charred because people didn't think a forest fire would reach them. Drivers dead because they thought alcohol wouldn't affect them.

They were overwhelmed. They underestimated the danger.

You would never do that. Or would you?

If anyone had a right to say "I'm too smart for that," it was Solomon, the wisest man in the world (1 Kings 3:12) and the son of Israel's most godly king. Yet Solomon's foreign wives pulled him into what he knew was wrong. He built temples to foreign gods, where idols were worshiped through prostitution and child sacrifice. Even Solomon wasn't smart enough. He listened to lies. He lost his love for God.

You're surrounded by a world that tells you lies, pulling you from God and His ways: *Adults are stupid. Money equals happiness. Trendy clothes and a perfect body make you supreme. Sex is a sport without rules. Treating people like trash doesn't stink.*

You want to think that the voices thumping your ears and images poking your eyes don't affect you, that you're wise enough to outwit them. But as soon as you think you're that smart, be sure of one thing: You'll find out quickly how stupid you can be (1 Corinthians 10:12).

As Solomon grew old, his wives turned his heart after other gods, and his heart was not fully devoted to the Lord *his God, as the heart of David his father had been.*

1 Kings 11:4

46
Morning Breath

You wouldn't think of facing your friends without scrutinizing your looks in a mirror. You inspect your hair (to decide if it's a hat day). You search for facial fuzz and ponder whether to save it or shave it (unless you're a girl—then you scream). You take a pimple population census (to determine whether to go back to bed).

What you see in the mirror in the morning—good, bad, or utterly ugly—is seared in your brain for the rest of the day.

Looking in the mirror is a serious endeavor. And you don't just gawk. When your breath creates a green fog on the mirror, you make friends with your toothbrush. When light glares off your shiny nose, you get chummy with the soap. When your hair looks like your mom's high-school graduation photo, you get a grip on a blow-dryer and start repairing.

Basically, you do something about what you see.

☑ **Read James 1:22–25. What does it mean to really pay attention to God's words?**

Hearing God's voice by reading the Bible is like looking in a mirror that reflects perfectly everything you need to see about yourself and your world—what's great and what needs to change. God's Word lets you see yourself and everything else as God sees it: truthfully.

But *hearing* is only the first part of listening to God. *Doing* is the second part. Paying attention to God means looking into the mirror of God's Word and responding to what you see. When you *listen* and *do* you will "be blessed." You'll find safety and freedom as you stay close to God.

God is the one Being in the universe who is totally powerful, totally smart, and totally loving. He's the One you can trust to be totally honest with you.

He's the One to listen to. And He's the One to obey.

Do not merely listen to the word, and so deceive yourselves. Do what it says.

JAMES 1:22

Acknowledgments

Thank you to my wife, Lyn. Thanks for choosing to follow Christ with me for twelve years and for being so good at hearing His voice. It's great to be in love with you.

Thanks to Nathaniel and Karin for being happy when Daddy comes home.

Thanks to our parents, Roy and Lois Johnson and Tom and Pat Benson. Your creaking 30-year-olds still need you very much.

Thank you to Elmbrook's 6th-8th graders, their parents, and my leaders, for so abundantly supplying ideas for writing. Names have usually been changed to protect the innocent (and the guilty!)

Thanks to Barb Lilland and Bethany House Publishers for their flexibility, kindness, and support with this series.

And thank you to the leadership of Elmbrook Church—the elders, and Stuart Briscoe, Mel Lawrenz, and Dick Robinson—for giving me freedom to write and study.

To God's Glory,
Kevin Walter Johnson